Wild Britain

Herring Gull

Louise and Richard Spilsbury

www.heinemann.co.uk
Visit our website to find out more information about Heinemann Library books.

To order:
☎ Phone 44 (0) 1865 888066
📄 Send a fax to 44 (0) 1865 314091
🖥 Visit the Heinemann Bookshop at www.heinemann.co.uk to browse our catalogue and order online.

First published in Great Britain by Heinemann Library, Halley Court, Jordan Hill, Oxford OX2 8EJ, part of Harcourt Education Ltd. Heinemann is a registered trademark of Harcourt Education Ltd.

Editorial: Lucy Thunder and Helen Cannons
Design: David Poole and Celia Floyd
Illustrations: Jeff Edwards, Alan Fraser and Geoff Ward
Picture Research: Rebecca Sodergren and Peter Morris
Production: Edward Moore

Originated by Repro Multi-Warna
Printed and bound in China by South China Printing Company

The paper used to print this book comes from sustainable resources.

ISBN 0 431 03982 8
08 07 06 05 04
10 9 8 7 6 5 4 3 2 1

British Library Cataloguing in Publication Data
Spilsbury, Louise and Spilsbury, Richard
Herring gull. – (Wild britain)
598.3'38'0941

A full catalogue record for this book is available from the British Library.

Acknowledgements

The Publishers would like to thank the following for permission to reproduce photographs:

Ardea/J.B. & S. Bottomley p25; Ardea/Bill Coster p14; Ardea/Paul Germain p10; Ardea/Geoff Trinder p22; Ardea/David & Katie Urry p19; Bruce Coleman/Colin Varndell p5; Corbis/Lynda Richardson p24; Corbis/D. Robert & Lorri Franz p26; Environmental Images/David Hoffman p9; ePics Scotland p27; FLPA/H. D. Brand 1 p20; FLPA/David Hosking p15; FLPA/E. & D. Hosking pp12, 28; FLPA/M. Jones p17; FLPA/A. Wharton p21; FLPA/R. Wilmshurst p16; Mark Hamblin/RSPCA Photolibrary p23; NHPA/Jim Bain p18; NHPA/Bill Coster p8; Oxford Scientific Films/David Cayless p6; Oxford Scientific Films/Chris Knights p11; Oxford Scientific Films/Richard Packwood p13; Oxford Scientific Films/Eric Woods p29; PPL p4.

Cover photograph of a herring gull on a rock by the sea, reproduced with permission of FLPA/M. B. Withers.

The Publishers would like to thank Michael Scott for his assistance in the preparation of this book.

Every effort has been made to contact copyright holders of any material reproduced in this book. Any omissions will be rectified in subsequent printings if notice is given to the Publisher.

Contents

Any words appearing in the text in bold, **like this**, are explained in the Glossary.

What are herring gulls?

When people talk about seagulls they usually mean herring gulls, like this one.

Gulls are large **seabirds**. There are several different kinds of gull in Britain. Herring gulls are the most common. There are about 300,000 herring gulls in Britain!

Adult herring gulls are about 60 centimetres long.

Herring gulls have a white head and belly and a grey back and wings. They have black **wing tips** and pink legs and feet. Their **beaks** are yellow.

Where do herring gulls live?

When herring gulls come ashore, some live in towns and cities. They sit on roofs instead of cliffs.

Most herring gulls spend their time at sea or by the coast. When they come to shore they live on seaside cliffs and beaches. Some herring gulls live inland by lakes or **marshes**.

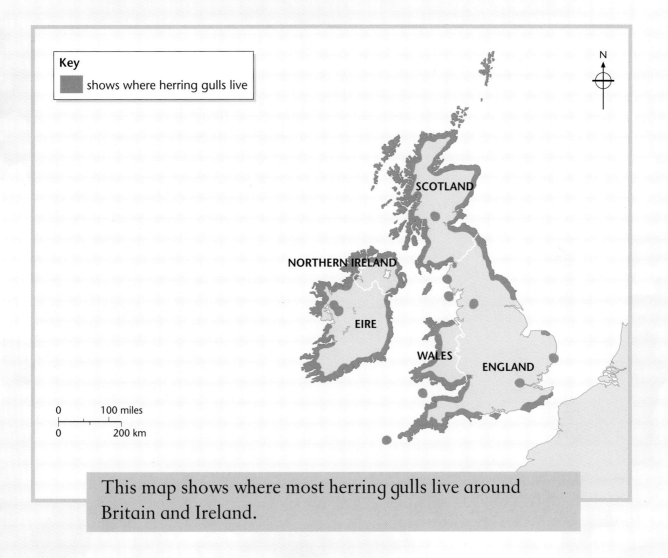

Key
■ shows where herring gulls live

SCOTLAND

NORTHERN IRELAND

EIRE

WALES

ENGLAND

N

0   100 miles
0   200 km

This map shows where most herring gulls live around Britain and Ireland.

When herring gulls fly out to sea, they do not go very far from land. Along the coasts of Britain, Ireland and the rest of Europe, you can see herring gulls all year round.

7

What do herring gulls eat?

Herring gull is not a very good name for this bird. It eats lots of different kinds of fish and other food, not just herrings!

On the seashore, gulls eat lots of different kinds of food. They eat worms, fish, crabs, young birds and **eggs**. Their curved **beaks** help them hold wet, slippery food.

These herring gulls are feeding on food scraps at a rubbish tip.

Herring gulls help to keep beaches clean by eating dead fish and other **waste**. They also eat scraps of food from rubbish tips or bins.

Finding food

When herring gulls spot food from above, they swoop down and catch it in their **beaks**.

Herring gulls have very good eyesight. In fact, they can see seven times better than we can! They spot food on sea or land from high in the sky.

When a plough turns over the soil, gulls catch the worms that come to the surface.

Herring gulls follow fishing boats to eat any small fish that fishermen throw back in the sea. They fly behind ploughing tractors to find worms.

On the move

Herring gulls have long wings to help them fly.

Herring gulls fly quite quickly. They can also glide with their wings still. Draughts of rising air help to hold them up, without them having to flap their wings.

A herring gull's webbed feet help it to walk and swim.

On water, gulls paddle along using their **webbed feet**. They also use their feet to stamp up and down on sand. This makes worms come to the surface!

Resting and nesting

This herring gull is taking a rest from flying. It is sitting in the gently rolling water.

Herring gulls can rest and sleep on the rolling waves out at sea. Sometimes they fly in to land for a few hours or for a night. They rest on rocky ledges or buildings.

Herring gulls often return to the same place every year to make their nests.

Seabirds must come to shore to make **nests** to lay their **eggs** in. Herring gulls often gather in big groups at nesting time. Each set of parents has their own nest area.

A herring gull's nest

Herring gulls often make nests high up so **predators** cannot reach the eggs.

Herring gulls make their **nests** on flat grassy ledges on sea cliffs. They also build nests on rocky islands, **sand dunes** or even rooftops.

Female herring gulls usually lay three eggs in their nests.

Both parents help to build the nest. They make it out of dry grass or seaweed. They line it with feathers. Herring gulls make round nests with a rim to hold the **eggs** in.

Young herring gulls

Baby herring gulls use their strong beaks to help them break out of their eggshells.

Both parents take turns to sit on the **eggs**. This keeps the eggs warm so the baby birds grow inside. The **chicks hatch** out of the eggs after about four weeks.

Herring gull chicks are covered in fluffy feathers, called down. Down keeps them warm.

Herring gull chicks eat soft fish that their parents have chewed for them. The baby taps the red spot on its parent's **beak** to ask for food.

Growing up

Parents use their wings to scare off other herring gulls.
Chicks can be eaten if they are not guarded carefully.

After a few days **chicks** start to walk about. Their parents watch them carefully as they wander around. Chicks start to fly by the time they are six weeks old.

Young herring gulls have speckled brown feathers and a black **beak**.

A young herring gull leaves its parents at about two months old. It catches its own food. It becomes an adult at four years old. Then it can have young of its own.

Herring gull sounds

Herring gulls often squawk to ask picnickers for food. It is best not to feed gulls.

Herring gulls make different sounds. One call warns other birds of danger. Young gulls whine when hungry. A loud ringing call means a gull is ready to fight.

Gulls may also squabble noisily over food!

Herring gulls make most noise when it is nesting time. Adult gulls squabble over nesting areas. One herring gull gives a long trumpeting call to tell others to keep out!

Under attack

Herring gulls can be very fierce when they are protecting their nests.

Predators, such as foxes, rats or other gulls, eat herring gull **eggs**. Some eggs are washed away by storms. If eggs are lost, gulls often lay another set in the **nest**.

If a young herring gull is born in a nest in a city it usually returns there to have its own young.

Herring gulls may make nests in cities because there are fewer predators to eat their eggs. If herring gulls survive their first year, they may live to be over 25 years old.

Gulls and people

Herring gull **droppings** make a mess on roofs and cars.

Herring gulls help us by keeping beaches clean, but they can be a nuisance. Parent gulls may swoop on people to keep them away from their **nests**.

Herring gulls can become a nuisance when they gather at seaside towns to feed.

In towns near the coast there are signs telling people not to feed gulls. In many places herring gulls have begun to steal food from people's hands.

A gull's year

Herring gulls have their young in summer when it is warm and there is plenty of food about.

Herring gulls arrive at their nesting area in spring. They find a partner and build a **nest** together. A pair of herring gulls usually has only one family of **chicks** a year.

Birds need clean healthy feathers to keep them warm and to help them fly.

Herring gulls **moult** throughout the summer. Their old feathers gradually fall out. New feathers grow in their place. These new feathers help to keep them warm in winter.

Gulls in Britain

All gulls are **seabirds** with long wings.
There are five birds called gulls in Britain.
What differences can you see between
these three and the herring gull?

lesser black-backed gull

common gull

black-headed gull

The artwork on this
page is not to scale.

Glossary

beak   hard, pointed part of a bird's mouth

chick   young bird that is not yet fully grown and able to fly

droppings   bird droppings are a mixture of urine (wee) and faeces (poo)

eggs   the young of some animals grow inside eggs until they are ready to hatch out

female   animal which can become a mother when it is grown up. A female human is called a woman or girl.

hatch   to come out of an egg

marshes   area of wet land, such as you find by the edge of an estuary or stream

moult   when an animal loses its old coat of feathers or hair and grows a new one

nest   somewhere safe for a bird to lay its eggs

predator   animal that catches and eats other animals for food

sand dunes   small hills of sand that pile up behind a beach

seabirds   birds that usually spend most of their time at sea or by the coast

waste   waste on a beach can be dead animals, rubbish thrown from boats or food dropped by people

webbed feet   animals' feet with skin between the toes, used for swimming and paddling

wing tips   pointed ends of a bird's wings

Index